This book belongs to …

....

Six in a Bed and Other Stories

How this collection works

This *Read with Biff, Chip and Kipper* collection is the second in the series at Level 1. It is divided into two distinct halves.

The first half focuses on phonics-based reading practice, with two reading and activity books, *Biff's Wonder Words* and *Floppy's Fun Phonics*. The second half contains four separate *Stories for Wider Reading* that use everyday language: *Floppy Did This!*, *Who is it?*, *Six in a Bed* and *Get Dad!* These stories help to broaden your child's wider reading experience. There are fun activities to enjoy throughout the book.

How to use this book

Find a time to read with your child when they are not too tired and are happy to concentrate for about ten minutes. Reading at this stage should be a shared and enjoyable experience. It is best to choose just one of the activity books or one of the *Stories for Wider Reading* for each session.

There are tips for reading together for each part of the book. The first tips are on pages 6 and 28. They show you how to introduce your child to the phonics activities. Tips to tell you how you can best approach reading the stories with a wider vocabulary are given on pages 50 and 72.

Enjoy sharing the stories!

The **Helping Your Child to Read** handbook contains a wealth of practical information, tips and activities.

OXFORD
UNIVERSITY PRESS

Great Clarendon Street, Oxford, OX2 6DP, United Kingdom

Oxford University Press is a department of the University of Oxford.
It furthers the University's objective of excellence in research, scholarship,
and education by publishing worldwide. Oxford is a registered trade mark of
Oxford University Press in the UK and in certain other countries

ISBN: 978-0-19-279398-0

5 7 9 10 8 6

Typeset in Edbaskerville

Paper used in the production of this book is a natural, recyclable product made
from wood grown in sustainable forests. The manufacturing process conforms
to the environmental regulations of the country of origin.

Acknowledgements;
Series Editors: Kate Ruttle, Annemarie Young

READ WITH
Biff,
Chip &
Kipper

Six in a Bed
and Other Stories

Phonics

Stories for Wider Reading

OXFORD
UNIVERSITY PRESS

Tips for Reading Biff's Wonder Words

Children learn best when they are having fun.

- Tell your child they are going to help Biff to read words and play 'I Spy'.

- Ask your child to read each of the words on the left hand page. Then ask them to find them in the scene on the right hand page.

- Once they have done this, ask them to do the activity on the right hand page: find objects where the words start or end with a particular letter, or find words that rhyme.

- Don't forget that when you talk about letter sounds, for example 'b', you say *buh* not *bee*. You can listen to the letter sounds on www.oxfordowl.co.uk.

- Give lots of praise as your child plays the game with you.

- Do the odd one out puzzle on each page and the spot the difference activity on page 26.

Have fun!

Find the odd one out on every left hand page.

This book practises these letter sounds:
s a t p i n m d g o c k ck e u r h b f ff ll ss

For more hints and tips on helping your child become a successful and enthusiastic reader look at our website www.oxfordowl.co.uk.

Biff's Wonder Words

Help me read these words.
Can you find them in the picture?

Mum
Dad

dog, duck, door, drum, duckling, dandelion

8

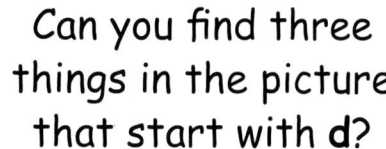

Can you find three things in the picture that start with **d**?

 Read these words and find them in the picture.

dog

cat

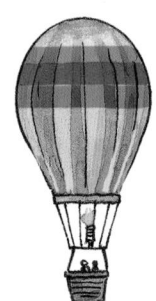

log, frog, bog

10

 Read these words and
find them in the picture.

mud

cap

web

water, wind, woodpecker

Read these words and
find them in the picture.

bag

hat

pen

nut, mat, cat

14

 Read these words and find them in the picture. Which words rhyme?

man

bus

cab

van

can, pan

 Read these words and find them in the picture.

sun

cup

jam

log

Chip, cup, sheep

Can you find three things in the picture that end with **p**?

Read these words and find them in the picture. Which words rhyme?

hen

bug

leg

den

den, pen

20

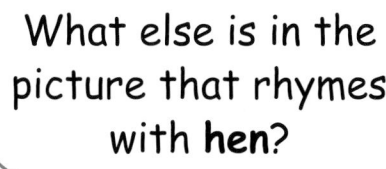

What else is in the picture that rhymes with **hen**?

Read these words and
find them in the picture.

mop

pot

mug

lid

tap

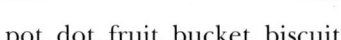
pot, dot, fruit, bucket, biscuit

22

How many things can you find that end in **t**?

 Read these words and find them in the picture.

Biff

rug

bed

mess

sock

clock, mug, head

25

Spot the difference

Find the five differences in the two pictures of Biff.

Tips for Reading Floppy's Fun Phonics

Children learn best when reading is fun.

- Tell your child they are going to play a more difficult game of 'I Spy'.

- On each page, read the instruction aloud, then ask your child to read the phrases on the left hand pages and try to match them to the pictures on the right.

- Encourage your child to sound out the letters and say the words (e.g. *l-i-d lid*)

- Your child will have to read carefully because some of the pages are tricky! Give them lots of praise.

- Do the odd one out activity on every left hand page and the spot the difference activity on page 48.

Have fun!

Find the odd one out on every left hand page.

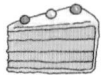

This book practises these letter sounds:

s a t p i n m d g o c c k e u r h b f ff ll

For more hints and tips on helping your child become a successful and enthusiastic reader look at our website www.oxfordowl.co.uk.

Floppy's Fun Phonics

Read the sentence on this card. Which picture matches the card?

Dad is sad.

31

Read the captions on these cards. Which card matches the picture?

rats on a sack

cats on a sock

32

Read the captions on these cards. Which card matches the picture?

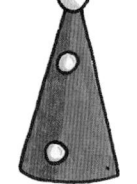

a hen and a bug

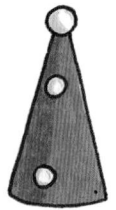

a hat on a dog

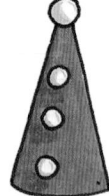

Read the sentences on these cards. Which card matches the picture?

Run in the sun.

Sit in the sun.

Read the sentences on these cards. Which card matches the picture?

A dog can sit.

A dog can run.

38

Read the sentences on these cards. Can you match each card to its picture?

A dog is a pet.

The dog is wet.

41

Read the sentences on these cards. Can you match each card to its picture?

Run and hop.

Run to the top.

Read the sentences on these cards. Can you match each card to its picture?

Biff is on a mug.

It is a big red bug.

45

Read the sentences on these cards. Can you match each card to its picture?

Biff is in a sack.

A doll is in a backpack.

46

Spot the difference

Find the five differences in the two pictures of Floppy.

Stories for Wider Reading

Tips for Reading *Floppy Did This!* and *Who is it?*

These two stories use simple everyday language. Some of the words used are not decodable, but you can help your child to read them in the context of the story.

- For each story, talk about the title and look through the pictures, so your child can see what the story is about.

- Read the story to your child, placing your finger under each word as you read.

- Read the story again and encourage your child to join in.

- Give lots of praise as your child reads with you.

- Talk about the story and do the fun activity at the end of each story.

Children enjoy re-reading stories and this helps to build their confidence.

Have fun!

After you have read *Floppy Did This!* find the paintbrush in each picture.

This book includes these useful common words:

it   is   no

50

Floppy Did This!

Chip did this.

It is Biff.

Biff did this.

It is Kipper.

Kipper did this.

It is Mum.

Oh, no!

Floppy did this!

Talk about the story

Who drew a picture of Kipper?

Why are they all clapping Floppy?

Which picture do you like best?

Who have you drawn pictures of?

Spot the difference

Find the five differences in the two pictures of Kipper.

Who Is It?

Who is it?

It is Kipper.

Who is it?

It is Biff.

Who is it?

It is Chip.

Is it Kipper?

No. It is Floppy!

Talk about the story

What was Kipper dressed up as on page 62?

What was Biff doing on page 63?

What was the trick on page 67?

What do you like dressing up as?

Twins

Find the twin clowns.

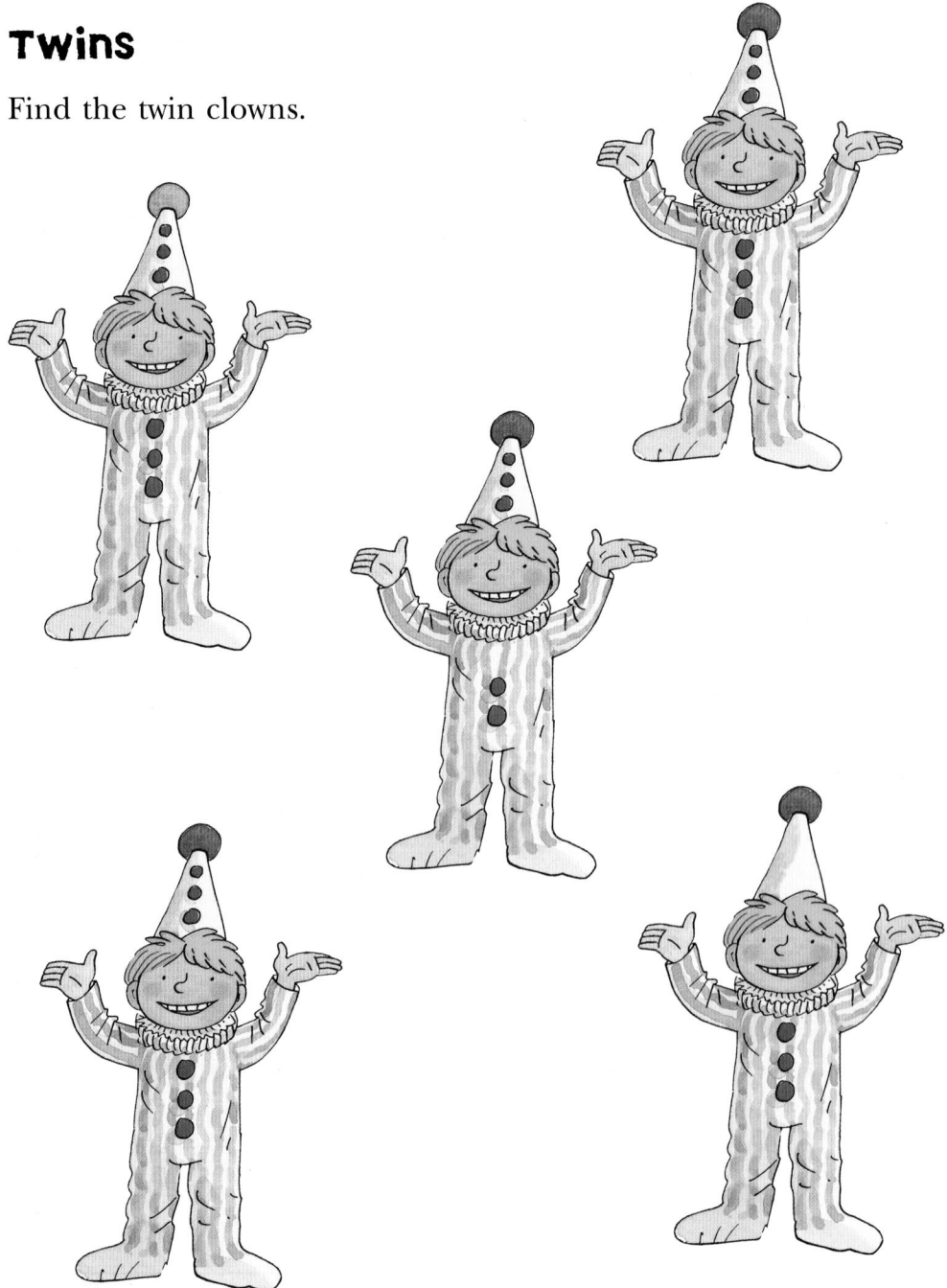

Tips for Reading *Six in a Bed* and *Get Dad!*

These two stories use simple everyday language. Some of the words used are not decodable, but you can help your child to read them in the context of the story.

- For each story, talk about the title and look through the pictures so your child can see what the story is about.

- Read the story to your child, placing your finger under each word as you read.

- Read the story again and encourage your child to join in.

- Give lots of praise as your child reads with you.

- Talk about the story and do the fun activity at the end of each story.

Children enjoy re-reading stories and this helps to build their confidence.

Have fun!

After you have read *Get Dad!* find the butterfly in each picture.

This book includes these useful common words:
Mum Dad get on go

For more hints and tips on helping your child become a successful and enthusiastic reader look at our website www.oxfordowl.co.uk.

Six in a Bed

Mum and Dad.

Mum, Kipper and Dad.

Mum, Kipper, Dad and Chip.

Biff, Mum, Kipper, Dad, Chip…

...and Floppy!

Talk about the story

Who got into bed with Mum and Dad first?

What did Kipper take with him?

Why did Floppy join in?

What do you like to do with all of your family?

Matching

Match the people with their belongings.

Get Dad!

Go on, Dad!

Get Biff.

Go on, Dad!

Get Chip.

Go on, Dad!

Get Kipper.

Go on, Mum!

Get Dad!

Talk about the story

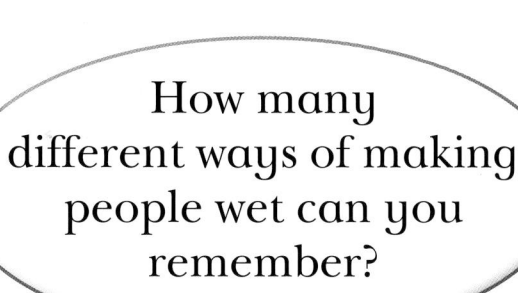

What did Dad use to spray Biff?

How many different ways of making people wet can you remember?

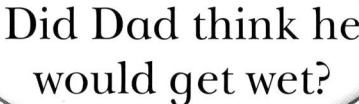

Did Dad think he would get wet?

What do you like to play when it's hot?

Maze

Help the children get to Dad.

The UK's best-selling home reading series

Phonics activities and stories help children practise their sounds and letters, as they learn to do in school.

Stories for wider reading have been specially written using everyday language to provide a broader reading experience for your child.

Level 1
Getting ready to read

Kipper's Alphabet I Spy · Chip's Letter Sounds · Biff's Wonder Words · Biff's Fun Phonics · Kipper's Rhymes · Floppy's Fun Phonics

Get On · Floppy Did This! · Up You Go · The Pancake · A Good Trick · Six in a Bed

Level 2
Starting to read

I am Kipper · Cat in a Bag · The Red Hen · Win a Nut · A Yak at the Picnic · The Fizz-Buzz

Funny Fish · Silly Races! · The Snowman · Mum's New Hat · Picnic Time · Dad's Birthday

Level 3
Becoming a reader

Such a Fuss · Shops · The Sing Song · The Backpack · Poor Old Rabbit · I Can Trick a Tiger · Super Dad · Floppy and the Bone

Level 4
Developing as a reader

Wet Feet · The Moon Jet · The Red Coat · Quick! Quick! · Missing! · Raft Race · Dragon Danger · The Spaceship

Level 5
Building confidence in reading

Egg Fried Rice · Craig Saves the Day · Seasick · Dolphin Rescue · Hungry Floppy · Husky Adventure · Trapped! · Looking after Gran

Level 6
Reading with confidence

Gran's New Blue Shoes · Ice City · Save Pudding Wood · Uncle Max · Hairy-Scary Monster · Mountain Rescue · The Lost Voice · Secret of the Sands

Read with Biff, Chip and Kipper Collections:

Up You Go and Other Stories · Kipper's Rhymes and Other Stories · Six in a Bed and Other Stories · Funny Fish and Other Stories · Picnic Time and Other Stories · The Fizz-Buzz and Other Stories · Floppy and the Bone and Other Stories

I Can Trick a Tiger and Other Stories · The Moon Jet and Other Stories · Dragon Danger and Other Stories · Husky Adventure and Other Stories · Looking After Gran and Other Stories · Hairy-Scary Monster and Other Stories · Secret of the Sands and Other Stories

Every collection includes phonics and stories using everyday language

Phonics support

Flashcards are a really fun way to practise phonics and build reading skills. **Age 3+**

My Phonics Kit is designed to support you and your child as you practise phonics together at home. It includes stickers, workbooks, interactive eBooks, support for parents and more! **Age 5+**

Read Write Inc. Phonics: A range of fun rhyming stories to support decoding skills. **Age 4+**

Songbirds Phonics: Lively and engaging phonics stories from former Children's Laureate, Julia Donaldson. **Age 4+**

Helping your child's learning with free eBooks, essential tips and fun activities

www.oxfordowl.co.uk

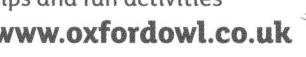